Sports Illustrated KIDS

STARS OF SPORTS

TRAVIS KELCE

SUPERSTAR TIGHT END

by Ryan G. Van Cleave

CAPSTONE PRESS
a capstone imprint

Published by Capstone Press, an imprint of Capstone
1710 Roe Crest Drive, North Mankato, Minnesota 56003
capstonepub.com

Library of Congress Cataloging-in-Publication Data
Names: Van Cleave, Ryan G., 1972- author. Title: Travis Kelce : superstar tight end / by Ryan G. Van Cleave.
Description: North Mankato, Minnesota : Capstone Press, 2025. | Series: Sports illustrated kids stars of sports
Includes bibliographical references and index. | Audience: Ages 8-11 | Audience: Grades 4-6
Summary: In high school, Travis Kelce played quarterback. In college, Kelce moved to the tight end position.
This move would set the path for his legendary career with the Kansas City Chiefs. Hard work, dedication,
and perseverance took Kelce from a third-round NFL draft pick to a record-setting star. Get all the details
about his impactful football career.—Provided by publisher
Identifiers: LCCN 2024010786 (print) | LCCN 2024010787 (ebook) | ISBN 9781669094319 (hardcover)
ISBN 9781669094265 (paperback) | ISBN 9781669094272 (pdf) | ISBN 9781669094296 (kindle edition)
ISBN 9781669094289 (epub) Subjects: LCSH: Kelce, Travis, 1989—Juvenile literature. | Kansas City Chiefs
(Football team)—Juvenile literature. | Tight ends (Football)—United States—Biography. | Football players—
United States—Biography—Juvenile literature. Classification: LCC GV939.K36 V36 2025 (print)
LCC GV939.K36 (ebook) | DDC 796.332092 [B]—dc23/eng/20240306
LC record available at https://lccn.loc.gov/2024010786
LC ebook record available at https://lccn.loc.gov/2024010787

Editorial Credits
Editor: Christianne Jones; Designer: Jaime Willems; Media Researcher: Svetlana Zhurkin; Production Specialist:
Whitney Schaefer

Image Credits
Associated Press: St. Joseph News-Press/Sait Serkan Gurbuz, 14; Getty Images: Andy Lyons, 13, Dilip Vishwanat, 17, Ezra
Shaw, cover, Jamie Squire, 5, 25, Jared Wickerham, 9, Jim McIsaac, 11, Joe Robbins, 19, Michael Reaves, 23, Mike Ehrmann,
21, Patrick Smith, 12, 18, Perry Knotts, 15, Randy Shropshire/Netflix, 7, Sarah Stier, 22; Newscom: MEGA/Image Press
Agency, 27, MEGA/TMX/KC Current, 26, picture-alliance/dpa/Arne Dedert, 28; Shutterstock: Alex Kravtsov, 1, EQRoy, 8

Source Notes
Page 6, "It was a competition . . ." Emily Weaver, "All About Travis and Jason Kelce's Parents, Ed and Donna Kelce," *People*,
January 18, 2024, https://people.com/sports/all-about-travis-jason-kelce-parents-ed-donna-kelce, Accessed
January 26, 2024.

Page 12, "Live with it . . ." Tom Kludt, "Travis Kelce Is Going for It," *Vanity Fair*, June 28, 2023. https://www.vanityfair.
com/news/2023/06/travis-kelce-is-going-for-it, Accessed January 26, 2024.

Page 12, "I owe him so much . . ." Chris Licata, "Chiefs' Travis Kelce Details Getting Kicked off College Football Team,"
Heavy. https://heavy.com/sports/kansas-city-chiefs/chiefs-travis-kelce-details-getting-kicked-off-college-
football-team, Accessed January 26, 2024.

Page 14, "I just hear my brother saying . . ." Colin McEvoy and Tyler Piccotti, "10 Things You Might Not Know About Travis
Kelce," Biography.com, November 15, 2023, https://www.biography.com/athletes/a45344438/travis-kelce-facts,
Accessed January 26, 2024.

Page 19, "I've watched him blossom . . ." Andy Reid, New Heights podcast, episode 38, May 11, 2023, https://www.
youtube.com/watch?v=yodKjUxwvMU&ab_channel=NewHeights, Accessed January 26, 2024.

Page 24, "When it's all said and done . . . " Colin McEvoy and Tyler Piccotti, "10 Things You Might Not Know About Travis
Kelce," Biography.com, November 15, 2023, https://www.biography.com/athletes/a45344438/travis-kelce-facts,
Accessed January 26, 2024.

Page 28, "I care about my career and legacy . . ." Tom Klundt, "Travis Kelce Is Going for It," *Vanity Fair*, June 28, 2023,
https://www.vanityfair.com/news/2023/06/travis-kelce-is-going-for-it, Accessed June 28, 2023.

TABLE OF CONTENTS

Words in **BOLD** are in the glossary.

THE CHIEFS' COMEBACK

The San Francisco 49ers looked dominant during most of Super Bowl LIV. In the third quarter, hope was fading for Travis Kelce and the Kansas City Chiefs. They were down 20–10. But the team didn't give up.

In the electrifying fourth quarter, Chiefs' quarterback Patrick Mahomes found his moment. He saw Kelce break free from his defender. Mahomes fired the ball to the end zone. Kelce snatched it out of the air.

Touchdown!

The crowd's cheers were deafening. Kelce's touchdown narrowed the 49ers lead to 20–17. It was the spark that ignited the Chiefs' comeback. Fueled by this momentum, the Chiefs scored twice in the final three minutes of the game. The Chiefs won, 31–20.

As confetti filled the air, Kelce celebrated. He was the difference maker in the game. He created an unforgettable highlight in Super Bowl history.

FACT

In 2020, it had been 50 years since the Chiefs had won a Super Bowl. They are now considered a **dynasty**, winning the championship in 2020, 2023, and 2024.

CHAPTER ONE

THE YOUNGER BROTHER

Travis Kelce was born October 5, 1989, in Westlake, Ohio. His dad, Ed, worked in sales. His mom, Donna, was a bank manager. His brother, Jason, was almost 2 years old when Travis was born. The brothers spent lots of time playing in the yard. According to Donna, Travis was always trying to keep up with Jason.

For the two brothers, everything was a competition. Their mom admitted, "It was a competition to see who could get to the table first, who could get to the front seat of the car . . . they egged each other on."

After they nearly hurt their dad during a fight, things changed. Both boys decided to keep their competitiveness on the sports fields after that.

>>> Travis and Donna at the premiere of the Netflix show *Quarterback*

At Cleveland Heights High School, Kelce made a name for himself in sports. He played football, basketball, and baseball. As quarterback, Kelce showed impressive arm strength and **agility**. He earned the respect of teammates and opponents.

His talent also caught the attention of college **scouts**. He had offers from Eastern Michigan, the University of Akron, and Miami University in Ohio. But the one that appealed most was the University of Cincinnati. That's where his brother played.

》》》 The University of Cincinnati

CHAPTER TWO

COLLEGE CHALLENGES

Kelce's journey at Cincinnati started with a challenge. He was a **redshirt** his first year, meaning he didn't play in games. He still practiced with the team. During this time the coaches saw his potential at a new position—tight end. The tight end serves as a receiver and a blocker.

Kelce embraced this change. He was able to showcase his natural talent. His size, speed, and exceptional catching ability quickly made him a standout player. However, Kelce failed a drug test his sophomore year. He was suspended for 12 months and lost his scholarship.

>>> Kelce running the ball against Rutgers

In a panic, Kelce called his dad. "Live with it," his dad said. "Grow from it. Learn from it." Taking these words to heart, Kelce committed to turning his life around. His brother played a big role in this turnaround. Jason convinced the coaching staff to give Travis another chance.

Brotherly Love

After Travis was kicked off the football team, Jason came to his rescue. He insisted they live together. They even shared a room! "I owe him so much credit for doing that and putting his name on the line for me to be able to finish my career at Cincinnati," Travis said. "It was something that I cherish so much that's hard to explain to people, to be honest."

>>> Kelce worked hard and became a team leader his senior year.

Kelce's senior year marked a dramatic shift. He became a team leader, setting records and impressing NFL scouts. During the three seasons he played at Cincinnati, the team boasted a 32–7 record. He set the school record for the most single-season receiving yards by a tight end, with a total of 722.

This period of Kelce's life was about more than sports. He learned how to balance football and life. He showed determination and dedication.

CHAPTER THREE

NFL JOURNEY

The Kansas City Chiefs selected Kelce in the third round of the 2013 NFL **draft**. He was picked 63rd overall. Because of Kelce's college trouble, coaches weren't sure about drafting him. Once again, Jason helped out.

When Andy Reid coached the Philadelphia Eagles, he drafted Jason. Reid was now the coach of the Kansas City Chiefs. When Reid called Travis on draft day, he asked to talk to Jason. "I just hear my brother saying, 'No coach, I got you.' I guess he told my brother, 'Make sure this kid doesn't screw this up for me.'"

〉〉〉 Kelce and Reid have built a strong relationship on and off the field.

Meaningful Number

Why does Kelce wear 87? Turns out, it's a tribute to Jason. He explained, saying, "If there is a Kelce **legacy**, two brothers making it to the NFL, it all started in 1987, because this big guy [his older brother, Jason] was born in 1987."

Unfortunately, Kelce's **rookie** season was difficult. A major knee injury meant he spent most of the season off the field. Kelce used this setback to his advantage. He learned from team veterans. He adjusted to the intensity and pace of the NFL.

A turning point came in 2014. Fully recovered, Kelce exploded on to the scene. He quickly established himself as a key player on the Chiefs' offense. That season, he recorded 67 receptions for 862 yards. He had five touchdowns. His playing style caught the attention of fans, players, and coaches. It was a mix of agility, strong receiving ability, and determination.

FACT

Kelce is known for his creative touchdown celebrations, which usually include dancing. He also has a signature move called the "Kelce Spike."

By 2016, Kelce reached a significant milestone. He had his first 1,000-yard season. He notched 85 receptions for 1,125 yards and four touchdowns. These stats made him one of the best tight ends in the NFL.

Kelce's dominance continued in the following years. He has not slowed down at all. Coach Reid has said, "I've watched him blossom into a leader . . . teammates love him."

〉〉〉 Kelce beats a defender and scores a touchdown.

CHAPTER FOUR

SUPER BOWL GLORY

Many great players never make it to a Super Bowl. So far, Kelce has played in four. The first was a win against the San Francisco 49ers in Super Bowl LIV in 2020. His critical touchdown in the fourth quarter was **pivotal** in clinching the victory.

The next year, in Super Bowl LV, the Chiefs faced the Tampa Bay Buccaneers. The Bucs were led by superstar Tom Brady. The Chiefs lost 31–9. However, Kelce's performance remained a highlight. He finished the game with 10 receptions for 133 yards.

FACT

Due to the COVID-19 pandemic, Super Bowl LV was played with limited attendance.

>>> Kelce had a stellar performance in his second Super Bowl.

In 2023, the Chiefs played the Philadelphia Eagles in Super Bowl LVII. Travis would face his brother. This was the first time brothers would play against each other on football's biggest stage. Travis recorded six receptions for 81 yards and a touchdown. The Chiefs defeated the Eagles 38–35 game.

In 2024, Super Bowl LVIII ended with a thrilling overtime win. The Chiefs beat the San Francisco 49ers 25–22. As usual, Kelce was the quarterback's favorite target. He caught nine of 10 passes for 93 receiving yards. The game added another chapter to Kelce's legacy. It also launched the Chiefs dynasty as they won back-to-back Super Bowls.

>>> Kelce was clutch during the second half of Super Bowl LVIII.

CHAPTER FIVE

LEAVING A LEGACY

Kelce's record-breaking performances speak volumes. In 2020, he set an NFL record for tight ends. He had 1,416 receiving yards in a single season. In 2022, he was the first tight end to go seven consecutive seasons with more than 1,000 receiving yards.

And with every game he plays, he seems to add more records to his name. Hall of Fame tight end Shannon Sharpe remarked, "When it's all said and done, I think you're going to have very little argument that he's the greatest tight end to play."

Kelce's personality captivates audiences in various media platforms. He discusses sports and life alongside his brother on the *New Heights* podcast. He hosted the TV show *Saturday Night Live* in 2023, showcasing his versatility and **charisma**.

FACT

Kelce is used to the spotlight. But that spotlight got a lot bigger in 2023 when he began dating superstar Taylor Swift.

Kelce's impact goes beyond the field. He loves helping his community. In 2015, he founded the Eighty-Seven & Running foundation. This charity helps underprivileged youth learn critical life skills through projects. The foundation creates safe, educational spaces for teens.

〉〉〉 Kelce brought his energy and dance moves to a charity event in 2023.

〉〉〉 Kelce loves showing off his personality through fashion.

Kelce has loved fashion since high school. In 2019, he launched his own clothing line. Tru Kolors reflects his personal flair and fashion-forward thinking.

"I like to show off who I am through what I wear," Travis says. "I think colors are a unique way to connect people and an amazing way to express yourself. We're all in this together—be you, stay true. And always rep your Tru Kolors."

Kelce's legacy is about moving forward as a dynamic athlete, a mentor, and an influential personality in sports and society.

"I care about my career and the legacy that I leave," he says, "but I do know that I have the opportunity to relate to a lot of people in this community. And with that, I think it's a bit of a responsibility to do the right things."

〉〉〉 Kelce speaks to the media during a press conference.

TIMELINE

1989 Born October 5 in Westlake, Ohio

2008 Graduates from Cleveland Heights High School

2008 Joins the University of Cincinnati Bearcats; redshirts first year

2010 Kicked off football team for failed drug test

2013 Drafted by the Kansas City Chiefs in the third round of the NFL draft

2013 Injures knee in preseason and is out most of the season

2014 Becomes a key player for the Chiefs

2015 Launches the Eighty-Seven & Running foundation

2016 Stars in the reality TV dating show *Catching Kelce*

2020 Sets an NFL record for receiving yards in a single season by a tight end

2020 Wins Super Bowl LIV versus the San Francisco 49ers

2021 Loses Super Bowl LV to the Tampa Bay Buccaneers

2022 Launches the *New Heights* podcast with his brother

2023 Faces his brother in Super Bowl LVII, winning 38–35

2024 Wins Super Bowl LVIII, in overtime, against the San Francisco 49ers

READ MORE

Anderson, Josh. *G.O.A.T. Football Tight Ends*. Minneapolis: Lerner Publishing, 2024.

Shulman, Mark and Solomon Shulman. *The Story of the Kansas City Chiefs*. Minneapolis: Kaleidoscope, 2020.

Stabler, David. *Meet Travis Kelce: Kansas City Chiefs Superstar*. Minneapolis: Lerner Publishing, 2024.

INTERNET SITES

Biography: 10 Things You Might Not Know About Travis Kelce
biography.com/athletes/a45344438/travis-kelce-facts

Kansas City Chiefs: Travis Kelce
chiefs.com/team/players-roster/travis-kelce

Kiddle: Travis Kelce Facts for Kids
kids.kiddle.co/Travis_Kelce

INDEX

AUTHOR BIO

Ryan G. Van Cleave is the author of dozens of books for children and hundreds of articles published in magazines. As The Picture Book Whisperer, they help celebrities write books for children. Ryan lives in Florida.